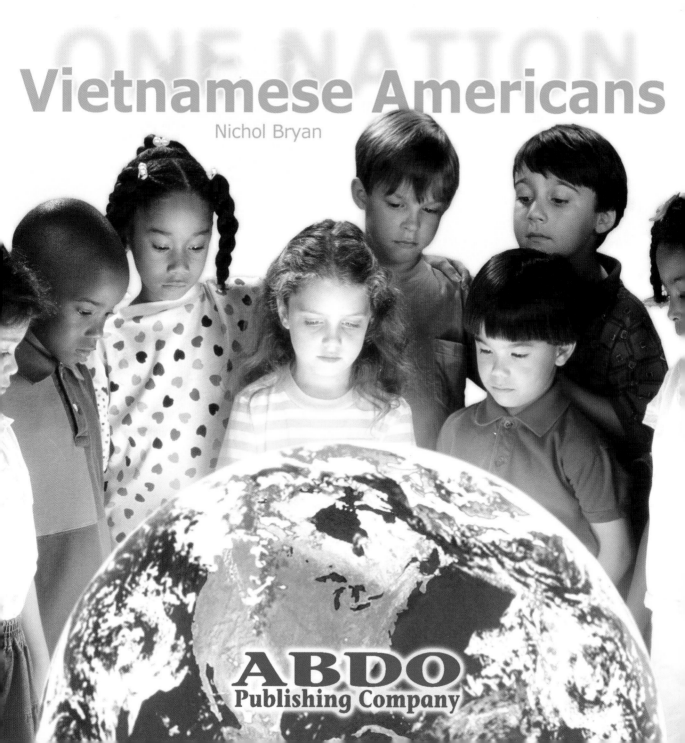

ONE NATION

Vietnamese Americans

Nichol Bryan

ABDO
Publishing Company

visit us at
www.abdopub.com

Published by ABDO Publishing Company, 4940 Viking Drive, Edina, Minnesota 55435.
Copyright © 2004 by Abdo Consulting Group, Inc. International copyrights reserved in all
countries. No part of this book may be reproduced in any form without written permission from
the publisher.

Printed in the United States.

Cover Photo: Corbis
Interior Photos: AP/Wide World pp. 8, 13; Corbis pp. 1, 2-3, 6, 7, 9, 10, 12, 15, 17, 19, 22, 23,
      25, 27, 30-31; Getty Images p. 28; Kayte Deioma pp. 5, 20, 21

Series Coordinator: Jennifer R. Krueger
Editors: Kristianne E. Buechler, Kate A. Conley
Art Direction & Maps: Neil Klinepier

All of the U.S. population statistics in the One Nation series are taken from the 2000 Census.
Special thanks to Hannah Nguyen for help with the Vietnamese language.

Library of Congress Cataloging-in-Publication Data

Bryan, Nichol, 1958-
    Vietnamese Americans / Nichol Bryan.
        p. cm. -- (One nation)
    Includes index.
    Summary: Provides information on the history of Vietnam and on the customs, language,
religion, and experiences of Vietnamese Americans.
    ISBN 1-59197-534-4
      1. Vietnamese Americans--Juvenile literature. [1. Vietnamese Americans. 2. Immigrants.]
I. Title.

E184.V53B79 2004
973'.049592--dc22   2003056268

Contents

Vietnamese Americans

Most Americans have ancestors who came from other countries. In fact, many Americans have come from other countries themselves. America is a collection of different **immigrant** groups. They began arriving after Christopher Columbus, an Italian explorer, traveled to the New World.

These immigrants have shaped the history of America. In the 1800s and 1900s, people from all over the world reached America's shores. Very few of these early immigrants were from Vietnam.

That began to change in the 1970s. After decades of war, many Vietnamese left their homes. They were seeking safety and a better life. Many immigrants found both when they moved to the United States.

In the United States, Vietnamese immigrants found an unfamiliar landscape and **culture**. They faced many hardships. But, with hard work and determination, these immigrants have started over as Vietnamese Americans.

Vietnamese-American children celebrate at a Tet festival in California.

Land of Legend

Vietnam is a long, narrow country in Southeast Asia. It stretches along the coast of the South China Sea. Legend states that the people of Vietnam **descended** from a dragon, Lac Long Quan, and Princess Au Co. They had 100 sons who were the first Vietnamese people.

Little is known about ancient Vietnam. Many believe that it had a strong **culture** before the Chinese conquered the country. When this happened in the 100s BC, Vietnam became a province of China. The Vietnamese regained their independence in AD 939. Vietnam once again became a strong country that spread its culture throughout the region.

But, Vietnam would not remain free. In the late 1800s, France conquered the

The yellow dragon is Vietnam's national symbol. Its color represents royalty.

Vietnam shares the Red River with China, its northern neighbor.

country. France ruled it as a colony until 1940. That year, Japan took over Vietnam. During Japanese rule, a group called the Vietminh fought the Japanese invaders. Their leader, Ho Chi Minh, wanted Vietnam to be an independent, **communist** country.

In 1945, the Japanese left Vietnam after their defeat in **World War II**. Ho Chi Minh still wanted Vietnam to become communist. But, the French did not want to lose Vietnam. They sent in troops and drove the Vietminh to northern Vietnam. Soon, Vietnam was split into two countries, north and south.

Ho Chi Minh

At this time, the United States wanted to stop communism from spreading throughout Asia. So, it tried to stop communist rule in Vietnam. To do this, the United States sent money to aid the French in their fight against the Vietminh.

But, the French could not defeat Ho Chi Minh's forces. So, the United States sent troops to help the South Vietnamese fight the North Vietnamese communists. During the war, millions of Vietnamese were killed. Others became **refugees** when their homes and villages were destroyed.

Heavy fighting in the Vietnam War forced these refugees to take cover in Hue, Vietnam, in 1968.

In the end, the **communist** troops held on. In 1973, the U.S. government decided to pull its troops from Vietnam. The government of South Vietnam collapsed. Vietnam was reunified under communist rule in 1975.

These events caused many Vietnamese to panic. They feared revenge from their new communist rulers. Many left the country to go to America, some in weak or damaged boats. They drifted across the China Sea.

These people often drowned or were attacked by pirates. The lucky ones reached a safe harbor or were taken aboard a friendly ship. Many of those who stayed behind were killed, or imprisoned in **re-education camps**.

Today, many Vietnamese struggle to make a living off the land in rural areas.

The Vietnam War changed Vietnam. The nation struggled with the loss of many lives. More than 30 years later, it is still working to rebuild. People have more freedoms today than when the **communists** first took over. But, jobs are few. In the countryside, half the people live in poverty.

The Journey from Vietnam to the United States

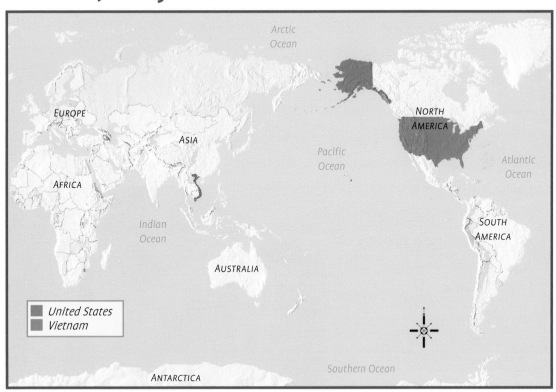

Safe Harbor

Very few Vietnamese **immigrated** to America until after the Vietnam War. Then the trickle of immigrants became a flood. Vietnamese desperately tried to escape their homeland. In the few months after the end of the war, 125,000 Vietnamese came to the United States.

The first immigrants from Vietnam were mostly educated professionals. They had worked in the government. Or, they had helped the United States in the war. The United States helped many of these people leave Vietnam. Many of them knew English and had little trouble finding jobs.

In the late 1970s and early 1980s, new groups of Vietnamese came to the United States. Some were people whose ancestors had come from China.

A U.S. ship evacuates Vietnamese refugees.

Many Vietnamese-American business owners display the South Vietnamese flag in memory of their homeland.

They had always faced **discrimination** in Vietnam. They were now the targets of revenge from the new **communist** government. More poor, uneducated farmers from the country began to escape.

The U.S. government felt responsible for the Vietnamese **refugees**. U.S. officials welcomed the refugees into military bases in California, Arkansas, Pennsylvania, and Florida. Some feared there were too many Vietnamese **immigrants** in those places. They thought there would not be enough jobs and resources in these communities to support them.

So, the U.S. government found other places for the Vietnamese to live. These places were spread out across the country. As a result, Vietnamese-American communities can be found all over the United States.

Vietnamese-American Communities

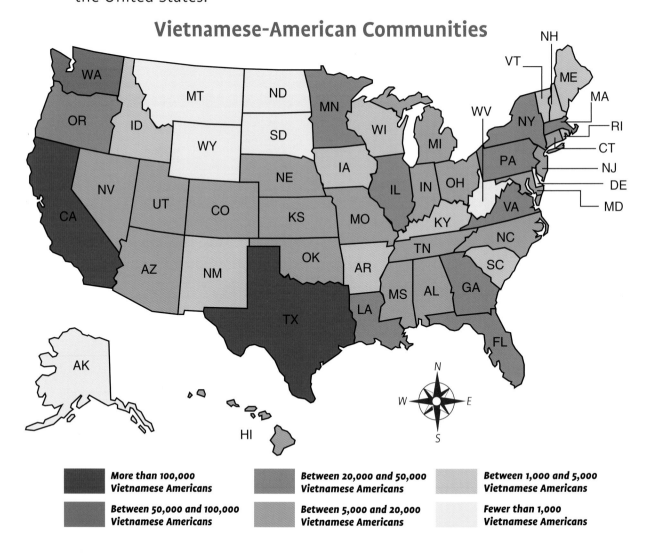

More than 100,000 Vietnamese Americans

Between 50,000 and 100,000 Vietnamese Americans

Between 20,000 and 50,000 Vietnamese Americans

Between 5,000 and 20,000 Vietnamese Americans

Between 1,000 and 5,000 Vietnamese Americans

Fewer than 1,000 Vietnamese Americans

After a while, many Vietnamese relocated to be with their families. Or, they moved to places where the climate was more like Vietnam's. Today, more than half of all Vietnamese Americans live in California and Texas.

Little Saigon is the largest Vietnamese-American community. It is an area in Westminster, California. Several thousand Vietnamese Americans live there. Little Saigon is also becoming a popular tourist attraction in California.

Little Saigon in Westminster, California

American life has been hard for some Vietnamese Americans. Those who came from rural Vietnam especially struggled. These **immigrants** had little money and spoke little English. They had few modern job skills. Many lived in poverty until they could find work.

Vietnamese Americans often faced **discrimination**. Many Vietnamese had helped the United States during the Vietnam War. Some Americans appreciated this. But, others treated the Vietnamese poorly because of their skin color or accent.

However, hard work and respect for education are important parts of the Vietnamese **culture**. These values helped Vietnamese Americans build a better life in the United States. Today, many work in professional, managerial, and high-tech jobs.

In the 1990s, the United States established better relations with Vietnam. This made it easier for the Vietnamese to immigrate. Because of this, a large percentage of Vietnamese Americans are newcomers to the United States.

Many Vietnamese-American families are still working to establish themselves. The adults often attend English language classes and special job skills courses. They do this to qualify for better jobs or for American citizenship.

Thousands of Vietnamese continue to **immigrate** to the United States every year. There are now more than 1 million Vietnamese Americans. They are one of the fastest growing groups of Asian Americans.

A Vietnamese man studies in a citizenship class. The class is held in Little Saigon of Westminster, California, where many Vietnamese Americans work to become citizens.

Becoming a Citizen

Vietnamese and other **immigrants** who come to the United States take the same path to citizenship. Immigrants become citizens in a process called naturalization. A government agency called the United States Citizenship and Immigration Services (USCIS) oversees this process.

The Path to Citizenship

Applying for Citizenship

The first step in becoming a citizen is filling out a form. It is called the Application for Naturalization. On the application, immigrants provide information about their past. Immigrants send the application to the USCIS.

Providing Information

Besides the application, immigrants must provide the USCIS with other items. They may include documents such as marriage licenses or old tax returns. Immigrants must also provide photographs and fingerprints. They are used for identification. The fingerprints are also used to check whether immigrants have committed crimes in the past.

The Interview

Next, a USCIS officer interviews each immigrant to discuss his or her application and background. In addition, the USCIS officer tests the immigrant's ability to speak, read, and write in English. The officer also tests the immigrant's knowledge of American civics.

The Oath

Immigrants approved for citizenship must take the Oath of Allegiance. Once immigrants take this oath, they are citizens. During the oath, immigrants promise to renounce loyalty to their native country, to support the U.S. Constitution, and to serve and defend the United States when needed.

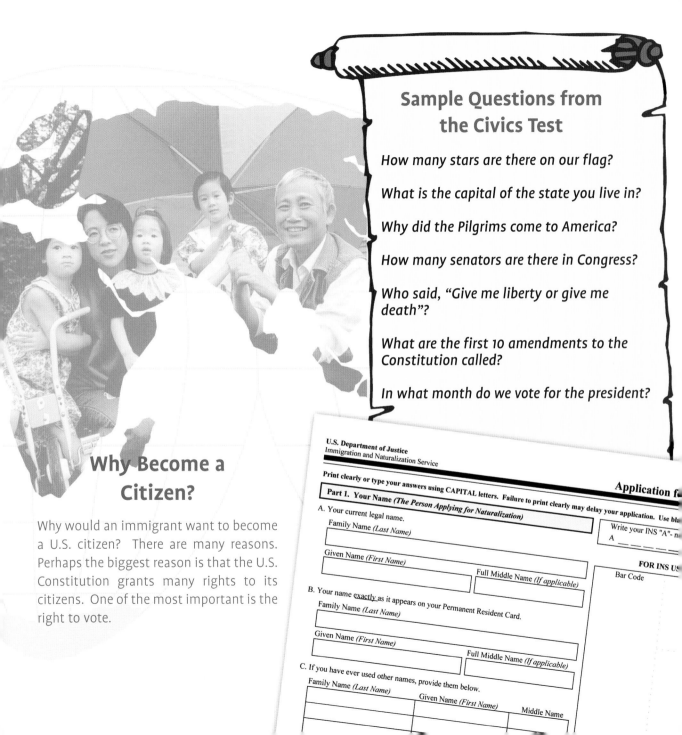

Sample Questions from the Civics Test

How many stars are there on our flag?

What is the capital of the state you live in?

Why did the Pilgrims come to America?

How many senators are there in Congress?

Who said, "Give me liberty or give me death"?

What are the first 10 amendments to the Constitution called?

In what month do we vote for the president?

Why Become a Citizen?

Why would an immigrant want to become a U.S. citizen? There are many reasons. Perhaps the biggest reason is that the U.S. Constitution grants many rights to its citizens. One of the most important is the right to vote.

U.S. Department of Justice
Immigration and Naturalization Service

Print clearly or type your answers using CAPITAL letters. Failure to print clearly may delay your application. Use bla

Application f

Part 1. Your Name *(The Person Applying for Naturalization)*

A. Your current legal name.

Family Name *(Last Name)*

Write your INS "A"- n
A _ _ _ _ _

Given Name *(First Name)*

Full Middle Name *(If applicable)*

FOR INS US
Bar Code

B. Your name <u>exactly</u> as it appears on your Permanent Resident Card.

Family Name *(Last Name)*

Given Name *(First Name)*

Full Middle Name *(If applicable)*

C. If you have ever used other names, provide them below.

Family Name *(Last Name)* | Given Name *(First Name)* | Middle Name

Way of Life

The Vietnamese had a lot to adjust to in their new homeland. They relied on each other for help. They also held on to their **culture** as a connection to their past. Today, they carry on traditions that are now Vietnamese American.

Many Generations

The family is central to Vietnamese culture. As many as five generations can share the same home. In the traditional family, the mother has most of the authority at home. The father has authority over decisions outside the home. Children are expected to live with their parents until they marry.

Today, Vietnamese-American children grow up in a different culture. They may not value the traditional Vietnamese family. This often puts younger Vietnamese Americans at odds with their elders.

A Vietnamese elder at a Tet celebration

Celebrate!

Vietnamese Americans have many colorful celebrations. The most important is Tet, the Vietnamese New Year. Tet is usually observed in late January or early February. It is a celebration of the new life that will come with spring. Vietnamese children especially like this holiday because they receive gifts of money.

Another important Vietnamese festival is the Mid-Autumn Festival. It's a day for children to get together and play games. They eat coconut cakes and have parades with lanterns. Many of these traditions are celebrated in places with large Vietnamese-American communities.

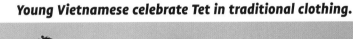

Young Vietnamese celebrate Tet in traditional clothing.

The Vietnamese make rice cakes, which are made of sweet rice, bean paste, and meat wrapped in banana leaves. Vietnamese Americans continue to make this traditional food in the United States.

Fish and Rice

Making and sharing food is a big part of Vietnamese **culture**. Fish is a major ingredient in their cooking. But, the Vietnamese depend on rice as the foundation of their diet.

Because they once ruled Vietnam, the French have influenced Vietnamese cooking. For example, Vietnamese meals often include asparagus and potatoes. These are not typical ingredients in other Asian foods. Vietnamese cooking also uses ingredients such as fish sauce, lime, and **cilantro**. These ingredients give Vietnamese cooking its own special flavor.

Eastern and Western Faiths

Many Vietnamese are Buddhists. Buddhism is based on the teachings of Siddhartha Gautama. He taught that suffering is caused by people clinging to possessions. Buddhists try to follow Buddha's teaching by **meditating** and living a good life. The goal of a Buddhist is to reach a state called *nirvana*, or "oneness with the universe."

A statue of Siddhartha Gautama, or Buddha, in Vietnam

Taoism is also an important religion among the Vietnamese. *Tao* is a word meaning "way" or "path." In Taoism, the Tao is the basic force behind nature and reality. Taoists try to be in harmony with the Tao. They do this through exercise and the study of nature.

Many Vietnamese Americans found a new faith in America. Christian churches in America were very active in helping recent Vietnamese **immigrants**. They helped them find jobs and homes. Because of that support, some Vietnamese immigrants became Christians.

Asian Language, Latin Letters

Vietnamese is a tonal language. It has six tones in all. The tone of the speaker's voice determines the word's meaning.

In written Vietnamese, each **syllable** has a special mark near its vowel. This mark shows which tone a speaker should use to say a specific word.

Traditional Vietnamese writing used Chinese-like characters. Later, French colonists developed a way to write Vietnamese using the Latin alphabet. This is the alphabet used to write French and English.

VIETNAMESE TONES

Mark	Tone	Meaning
ma	mid-level	ghost
má	high-rising	mother
mà	low-falling	which
mạ	low-rising	rice seedling
mả	low-broken	tomb
mã	high-broken	horse

The Vietnamese language uses the Latin alphabet, just like English.

Rising Stars

The Vietnamese have not lived in the United States as long as other **immigrant** groups. But, they have still made many contributions to American arts, entertainment, and society.

Tony Lam was the first Vietnamese-American elected official in the United States. In 1992, he became a councilman in Westminster, California. He overcame great obstacles to build a better future for his community. Over the years, he has worked hard to support Vietnamese-American **culture**.

Other Vietnamese Americans have made contributions in the arts. Tony Bui is a movie director. Bui was born in Saigon during the Vietnam War. He left with his parents for California shortly before the war's end. His award-winning movie, *Three Seasons*, is about what Vietnam is like today.

Another Vietnamese American in the arts is Khai Nguyen, a painter. Nguyen was born in Hue, Vietnam, in 1943. He escaped the **communist** regime in 1981. Nguyen has lived in California ever

Tony Bui (right) and actor Harvey Keitel at the American Film Festival

Dat Nguyen

since. In his art, he sometimes explores the relationship between humans and computers. He has won many awards for his artwork in Vietnam.

One Vietnamese American has even made great accomplishments in space! Eugene Trinh was born in Saigon and moved to the United States in 1968. Trinh followed his dream to fly in space. He became the first Vietnamese American to fly on NASA's **microgravity** laboratory space shuttle mission.

Another pioneer is Dat Nguyen. Nguyen was born in a **refugee** camp after his parents fled Vietnam in 1975. After graduating from college, he was **drafted** by the Dallas Cowboys. He was the first Vietnamese American to play in the National Football League. He was voted to *Football Digest's* All-Rookie Team after his first year.

Vietnamese Americans left behind a land torn apart by war. They came to a new country with a different language and **culture**. And, they faced many challenges. But with hard work and a love of learning, they have become successful Americans.

Glossary

cilantro - leaves of an herb used for flavoring in cooking.

communism - a social and economic system in which everything is owned by the government and is distributed to the people as needed.

culture - the customs, arts, and tools of a nation or people at a certain time.

descendant - a person who comes from a particular ancestor or group of ancestors.

discrimination - unfair treatment based on factors such as a person's race, religion, or gender.

draft - an event during which sports teams choose amateur players.

immigration - entry into another country to live. A person who immigrates is called an immigrant.

meditation - quiet, careful consideration and thinking.

microgravity - a condition of weightlessness experienced in space.

re-education camp - a place where prisoners are held and forced to work. Often, these prisoners are punished for opposing their government.

refugee - a person who flees to another country for safety and protection.

syllable - a single, uninterrupted sound.

World War II - from 1939 to 1945, fought in Europe, Asia, and Africa. The United States, France, Great Britain, the Soviet Union, and their allies were on one side. Germany, Italy, Japan, and their allies were on the other side. The war began when Germany invaded Poland. The United States entered the war in 1941 after Japan bombed Pearl Harbor, Hawaii.

Saying It

Au Co - OW CUH
Dat Nguyen - DAHT NWING
Ho Chi Minh - HOH CHEE MIHN
Khai Nguyen - KEYE NWING
Lac Long Quan - LAHK LONG KWUN
Saigon - seye-GAHN
Siddhartha Gautama - sihd-DAHR-tuh GOW-tuh-muh
Tao - DOW
Tony Bui - TOH-nee BOY
Vietminh - vee-EHT-MIHN

Web Sites

To learn more about Vietnamese Americans, visit ABDO Publishing Company on the World Wide Web at **www.abdopub.com**. Web sites about Vietnamese Americans are featured on our Book Links page. These links are routinely monitored and updated to provide the most current information available.

Index